ROBOTS

By Mike Artell

Illustrated by Ross Watton

Dominie Press, Inc.

Publisher: Raymond Yuen
Project Editor: John S. F. Graham
Editor: Bob Rowland
Designer: Greg DiGenti
Illustrator: Ross Watton

Published by:

꘡ Dominie Press, Inc.

1949 Kellogg Avenue
Carlsbad, California 92008 USA

www.dominie.com

1-800-232-4570

Paperback ISBN 0-7685-1823-7
Printed in Singapore
   11 12 13 14 V0ZF 14 13 12 11

Table of Contents

Chapter One
Robots Are Smart Machines

A machine is something we make to help us do work. Hammers and drills are simple machines. Computers and cars are machines that have many parts.

Machines help us do more work, or they make the work easier to do. Robots are machines that are controlled by computers. They do some of the things that humans can do, but robots can do them faster, better, and longer.

In 1920, a Czech man named Karel Capek wrote the first story about robots. The word *robot* comes from the Czech

word *robota*, which refers to certain days people had to work for no pay. In Karel's story, the robots look like people. They become evil and take over the world.

Maybe you have seen a movie with robots in it. Some robots in movies look like people. Robots that look like people are called androids.

Most real robots don't look like people. Some look like big arms with claws. Others look like little spaceships. There are even robots that look like insects.

Each robot is made to do a special job. Most robots do jobs that are dangerous, difficult, or boring for people to do.

Chapter Two
Robots Help with Work

When people build things, they sometimes have to do the same job over and over again. This is very boring work for human beings. But robots don't get bored. Robots are good at these kinds of jobs.

Robots can move heavy things and stack them. They can spray paint in the same spots without ever getting tired. Some robots even have powerful torches that can melt metals and join them together.

Not all robots build cars and other big machines. Some robots make cookies! One company uses robots to make its sandwich cookies.

The robots put the cookies together. Then they check to see if any of the cookies are broken or chipped. Finally, they put the cookies in bags. And the robots never sneak a snack.

Robots in the Military

The United States Army has robots that can fly. These robots look like small planes, but they don't have pilots inside to fly them. These flying robots can take pictures. They can also help protect soldiers.

The Army also has special robots that help soldiers on the ground. These robots have cameras, and they look like little cars. They move ahead of the soldiers to watch for danger.

Robots in Law Enforcement

"Bomb-bots" are robots that can find explosives. These robots can defuse bombs without putting police officers in danger.

The police can also send robots into dangerous situations where people might be shooting guns. The police can see people through the robot's camera. The police can talk with people and hear them, too.

Robots in Industry

Some robots can get into places where it would be impossible for people to go. One type of robot can roll along the insides of water and sewage pipes, looking for signs of damage. It has four-wheel drive, just like a truck, so it can move over and around obstacles, but it is only nine inches wide.

Demolition robots can be placed at certain locations in order to take down some parts of a building and preserve others. These robots are lighter, more maneuverable, and produce fewer pollutants than traditional demolition vehicles, like cranes and large trucks. They also help prevent damage to surrounding buildings from dust and falling debris.

Chapter Three
Robots in Science

Robots in Medicine

Doctors and hospitals also use robots. Robots help doctors work on parts of the body that are hard to reach.

The doctors use the robots and small video cameras to help with complicated operations. The robots are connected to computers, so the doctor can sit at a computer screen and perform an operation from another room.

If someone loses an arm or a leg in an accident, that person may be able to get robot arms or legs. These robot arms can help a person do many things and be more independent.

Robots in Exploration

Many robots are used for underwater exploration and scientific monitoring. These robots are used by oceanographers to go places that would be difficult for people to reach. Oceanographers are scientists who study the oceans and their effect on life on Earth.

One kind of robot, named Solo, operates close to the surface of the

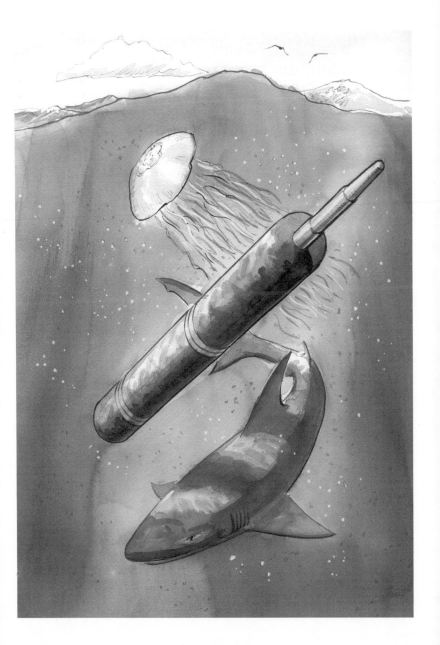

ocean, measuring the amount of carbon that plankton use. This robot has to both operate on its own and receive instructions by remote control from scientists. It sits in the ocean for months at a time, diving to different depths and gathering information. Every day it surfaces and points its antenna toward a satellite to transmit its collected data. The satellite then transmits this data to oceanographers.

Other underwater robots have arms that can move objects on the ocean floor and collect samples from areas that people would not be able to reach. Many of these robots are operated by scientists on board a boat on the surface of the water.

Chapter Four
Robots All Around Us

Robots in Education and Research

Many schools and colleges teach students how to build and program robots. The students study how to make robots better and easier to use.

The students build robots and test

them. Usually they work in groups. Each group comes up with its own design, and each design is different.

Some robots teach small children important ideas like fire safety. These robots are colorful and fun. They often look like cartoon characters.

Robots in Business and Entertainment

Some companies use robots to sell things. These robots have the name of the company on them. The robots make jokes and tell people about the company.

Restaurants and amusement parks use robots to entertain their customers. These robots look like they're talking and singing. Some of them even look like they're playing musical instruments.

The people who make movies often

build robots that look like animals. It's a lot easier to teach a robot cat to talk than to teach a real cat to talk!

Chapter Five
The Future of Robots

You will see a lot more robots in the future. Some will be large machines used in factories. Some will be small "insect-bots" that can crawl into tiny spaces.

Robots will continue to get smarter. Over time they will be able to do more

things without human help. Maybe one day there will be a robot that can clean your room for you!

Would you like to know more about robots?

Your library probably has many good books about robots. You can also search the Internet for information, stories, and even videos of robots in action. And check with your local bookstore, too.

Would you like to build and program robots for a living? If you like to work with computers, that's a good start. It also helps if you like mathematics. Get some paper and design your own robot!